Targeted Traffic Mastery

The Easy-to-Follow Guide to Buy

Targeted Traffic that Converts

Abraham Morris

All products are available for educational and informational purposes only. Nothing in my books, or any of my content, is a promise or guarantee of certain future results or earnings.

Table of Contents

Introduction

Exponential resource management is not just a fancy name. It is a really underestimated, under used marketing method that works incredibly well. So much so, this section is one of the main reasons we are only letting 500 copies of this go. I do not want my competition to be able to manage their customers correctly if it means I am going to get them instead.

What we are looking at here are your five primary resources, the lifeblood of any online business. That is your affiliates, your list, your customers, long-term customers, and joint venture prospects, all of which we will refer to from this point onwards as your resources, or your promotion power.

Each one of the big five have the power to make you sales, and thus big profits. However, imagine being able to take those five and manage them in such a way that you never have to carry out the expensive act of paying for new customers, a bigger, list, more affiliates or JV contacts ever again, but still having countless thousands of them flowing into your lap.

It sounds unthinkable, but with the right management of your resources, you are going to be seeing their usefulness double, multiply by three, four, sometimes even five.

What does this mean or your profits? Well, have you ever worked it out in your head how much you would make if you doubled a penny every day for a month or two?

The principal here is the same, but instead of money, you are using your resources. The more you have, the faster they build each other. The true power of real exponential growth is at every marketer's fingertips.

They just have to know how to realize it is there and understand how to use it to their advantage.

Overview of Resource Management

Part 1

❖ To demonstrate how to take your existing resources and cross them over in such a way that they begin to build themselves. The ultimate in marketing strategies allows you to boost your promotion power exponentially when others are having trouble even building a list that makes a single sale.

❖ To display a diagram to demonstrate this method helping you commit this to memory and act on your knowledge.

❖ To discuss each resource in depth and to define specific roles for each one, opening up ability to cross your resources and to start the snowball effect rolling.

- To avoid the pitfalls that other marketers are making as we speak with their crossing of resources if they have even discovered such a method in the first place.

- To inspire and to demonstrate ideas for the crossing of your resources, both enabling you to follow the examples we have laid out for you, and to come up with your own as your resources start to flood in when you launch your products.

Exponential Resource Management 1

Greetings, and welcome to manual entitled exponential resource management and treating your customers right. As well as a selection of literal ways to get the most out of your customers without giving them the earth for free, we will also be taking a little bit of a lateral detour here.

You see, when I say treating your customers right, I am not just talking about how to keep your customers happy.

Although this is important, what I am going to show you is much *more* important, and much more beneficial to you, and it should alter the way you think about what you are doing and how you are doing it.

Your five main resources: Joint Ventures, Affiliates, Standard List, Standard Customers, and Long-Term Customers.

That is exactly what this section is about. Not just being nice to people so they trust you more, we are going deeper than this to start with. We will leave the easier stuff until afterwards.

The Working Concept – An Overview

The whole idea of this section is based around kind of a cross promotion strategy, which is nothing new products wise, but when we look at it in terms of the five main resources you have been gathering it becomes a different matter entirely. What we are planning to do here is take the whopping promotion power of the big five, tie them together and double what they are doing for you without bringing in anyone new. We are simply referring each type of member to different sections.

Now, you may have seen this circle of five before when talking in terms of website promotion, using the site itself as a base to launch each resource onto the next stage in the ladder where possible, whilst at the same time bringing in new blood. This time around, we are taking that circle, and moving people around so that they can reside in multiple places, which in turn, can double, or even triple your promotion power simply because one person becomes two, three and up to five different resources on their own. Powerful stuff.

For quick reference, here is that basic resource circle that we are talking about. We will be adding to this in a moment.

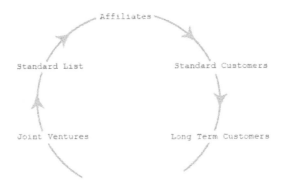

Now, this is going to become a big part of the circle, because it is going to add to it internally, as we are moving people around here without bringing in new people, increasing productivity of the people we already have, so please do take a careful look at it right now, or the rest of this section will not make any sense. The main thing I want you to keep in mind is the above diagram, as that will form the basis of your whole web-based marketing outlook. It will however be added to at the end of this manual, so that you have five large diagrams at the end of the course to base your marketing off of.

What we are going to do now is go through each resource and look at the most effective ways to cross them over to another resource, whether it is worth doing, why you should or should not do particular things with each section, most importantly, which ones are going to make you the most cash.

Even if you do not have all of these resources at your disposal yet, do not worry. The aim here is to show you what is going to go on when your promotions do go out and be prepared. Let me assure you, the speed that the five main resources come in may turn around and surprise you, It is going to come in very handy, very soon.

What to Do with Your List

So first up, let's start with your list. Think first about what your list is. It is your first contact, and it contains pretty much everyone that is passed through the system you have set up, from the freebie hunters to the people that did not know what they signed up for, those who had friends that signed them up for a joke, of course those who are going to progress through the circle and make you a whole load of cash in several different ways. It is the most numerous of all the five resources and is also in this instance of the lowest quality compared to the other four, however is essential if you want to fill the higher ranks.

An Important Tip

Keep in mind that it is not always possible or even in your best interests to subject a particular resource to this type of cross promotion. This is especially true for your more valuable money-makers.

The reason being is that they can be lost, just like any other resource, but when you take the regular customers who have spent many thousands of dollars on your products in small numbers, compared to a large list that have yet to spend, it is much more devastating to lose one or two percent of your big spenders than it is to lose one or two percent of your freebie seekers.

What to Do with Your List – Continued

So, getting started here, what do we want to turn your list into? Well, everything really. Your lists are there for one thing, and one thing only, and that is to act as your own media outlet and increase your other four resources (something that many businesses miss). Turning your list into customers and long-term customers is quite straight forward. You will be sending them announcements relating to your new products and services. It is as they should be used, and most often are.

Two more extremely profitable things that your list can do that people rarely ever seem to catch hold of (even more profitable than making direct sales) is build your affiliate base and on top of that build your joint venture base. First up, the affiliate building.

Remember I talked previously about promotion to build resources instead of making profits? Well, this works in exactly the same way. The reason we do not see it too often, aside from the people that have been told about it, or sussed it out already, is who in their right mind would promote, and in fact spend the two most important things (their money and their time) on promotion when they are not going to make any cash out of it directly.

The sooner that you, as a businessperson, online or offline can see how important it is to look beyond immediate profits from ad campaigns, the sooner you will start to make some real money. I guess it is overlooked by so many simply because in today's age of the internet, everyone wants something right now, they do not want to wait. The longer it takes to carry out, the more they overlook it as something that will not be an immediate fix for their situation.

Building Your Affiliates from Your List

One thing I do want to say to you now is, if you have sixty-five, seventy, eighty percent, or even more to give away through your products' commissions, do not be afraid to tell people about it. Not so long ago in fact, maybe two or three years prior to writing this report, there was a spate of big affiliate commission sites popping up that offered anywhere from 80-100% commissions that did incredibly well on the resource building side of things simply on the basis of promoting their high commissions more than the product itself.

So, whatever you do, do not think that gaining affiliates is all about that little button at the top of your sites with 80% for affiliates written in big letters.

Hey, we spend money to promote free products to build our lists all the time, why cannot we do the same for our affiliates? Well, we can, and to be honest, one good affiliate is more valuable than a hundred subscribers, even a thousand subscribers in my eyes, for the simple reason that they may have an audience of tens or even hundreds of thousands on their lists that they are willing to give you access to. Imagine the resources that would land in your lap and the power you will have for future promotion when a few ads like that start to go out.

So, the rule here is just this. If you are following the charts, we have put up for you, this guide, or a modified version of it, built around your own needs, and your commissions are higher than the average fifty percent, go ahead and make sure people know about it through your promotion. Make it a prime concern of yours and you will not be disappointed.

Turning Your List into Joint Ventures

Now as far as turning your list into joint ventures goes, this is a pretty easy but also open ended and rather variable in results until you actually see what these people are capable of further down the line. Similar to previously, when we talked about gaining feedback from your list you can in the same way, gain joint ventures from your list, again, as in above example with the affiliates, this is often far more widely used, and for good reason.

I urge you once again, not to relegate your joint venture prospects to those who visit your website, and the individuals you pick out through the top performing affiliates, but to actively seek them through your list. The reason we are doing this is simply because there is a good chance someone will be out there that will not progress down your line of resources otherwise. If they are experienced, have a big list of their own, or the ability to get in touch with your target market, you are going to miss out if you are not telling them that you want their services.

For example, an experienced marketer that subscribes to a selection of lists to keep up with what is going on around them, happens to subscribe to your list where you are selling an info product such as this. He or she will not buy your how-to product, because they've got their system set up already and it just so happens, that they only promote their own stuff to their own lists, unless it is a joint venture (this is very common among the big guys by the way), they will not buy your big product for the same reason, and they will not be joining your affiliate program for the above reason. He or she is a heavy hitter with a big list, but you are missing out. These are the people you are aiming to cater for here. It is not good if you are leaving massive holes like this, because you are missing out on some massive profit potential. In fact, as we speak the majority of marketers out there are very obviously leaving these types of holes.

The problem with joint venturing through a list at this stage is it becomes kind of a lottery if you are not careful. You cannot just send out a mailing asking for anyone with a list over ten thousand people to contact you for higher commissions, because then everyone else feels cheated and you may alienate some potential affiliates. In general terms joint ventures should be a private thing, the deal will also vary from person to person, depending on your product, their list size, what they want in return and what you can grant in return. The best way to go about this is to keep it that way. Do not do a mass mailing just requesting joint ventures for the reasons above, we cannot do that for this particular resource.

What I'd suggest you do instead, which you should be doing with your list anyway, is carry on as your normally do, sending out your un-intrusive surveys to help with your research and find out as much info as you can about the people on your list, for something in return. For example, a short valuable report that you have written on your area of expertise. In exchange you are getting vital info that not only allows you to tailor your ads to your list providing a better response rate, but at the same time you are building up a picture of who the good joint venture prospects are. Once you have done that, you can go through the results you have collected, and pick the top performers, the knowledgeable, and the people with the most resources, and contact them individually.

What to Do with Your List – Summary

So you see, your list is your first contact that you have with your customers and the potential is there to turn them into the other four resources further up the food chain if done as above. If it is related to your business, and other people should be seeing, reading, using, buying or promoting it, your list should know about it at least once, in it is unspecialized, most basic and standard form. Leave them in the dark, and you are missing out on potentially thousands, tens of thousands in profit, or more.

What to Do with Your Customers

Moving on from your list and your most general and untargeted form of targeted marketing, let's take a look at the first specialized section here, your customers. The people that have either only bought low priced introductory products from you before or have only purchased from you once.

What you will start to see is as we get more specialized and move up the food chain in terms of profitability, things start to get easier to figure out what to do and when to do it when crossing your resources over. It is also important to note, that with paying customers, and them being lower in numbers than your list, it is easier to make a mistake and lose profit potential rather quickly if you are not careful about where you are setting foot.

When thinking about what to do with what resource, remember to always think in terms of where these people are going next in the standard form when setting orders in the way of importance. For example, with our short-term customers, in the standard flow of things, they will be turning into your big buyers. The people that buy the most products from you at the highest price, so again, short term, they may not seem like much now, but in the future, this is where your big profits are going to be coming from, hence their major importance, and the general attitude is that you should give them something a little extra for their time. That is not because they are more demanding than your list, but because the profit potential is much higher for you, their numbers are much smaller, and the margin of error also is much smaller.

Organizing Is the Key to Success

Now, before we even start, we are seeing a new problem emerge. The organizing and managing of 5 different resources that all overlap can become a complex, time consuming and confusing task, and that is not what we want. I can rightly see why many just take all their five resources and just bundle them into one list. I would highly suggest you avoid doing this unless you are just promoting other people's stuff or very rarely create your own products. If your business is and will in the future remain all about the products you are creating and selling, keep them separate. If you carry this section out correctly, it will not mean a huge amount of extra work, aside from five short mailings per product promotion drive or launch instead of one.

Back to Managing Your Customers

The reason I mention the above is that when you get to this stage, the people out there that do things this way and keep their resources separated, try to give them the earth. For example, if I told you how valuable these people are, and you wanted to turn them into affiliates, how do you do so?

The general answer would be to give them higher commissions. This however is not worth your trouble, because we are overlooking one serious flaw in that plan. Unless your product is geared to give higher commissions in the beginning to people who purchase it, these people are not necessarily suited to affiliate material, and in my experience, it is best not to bombard them with affiliate signup pages and adverts about how much they can make unless that is a specific benefit of your product.

I would suggest to you that the only way around this is not to do the above, because your main aim is not to make them promote for you, but to buy your higher priced products and move up the ladder. So, the solution is treating them as such. When you are mailing them about a new product, include information about how much they can earn promoting for you.

I highly recommend not deviating from the original plan and flow of the chart with these important people, especially when it comes to trying to turn them into affiliates. You will gain plenty of them via the other resources, leave well alone trying to give them bonuses or bigger commissions at this stage, because otherwise you will just end up with a big, tangled ball of yarn and a headache. We will get on to just how we make them valued in a moment.

But first, let's look at turning your customers into your list. To start with, you will find that most of your customers are on your list anyway. Not much needs to be said about this subject for that very reason. Any customers that are not on your standard list will still be receiving ads for your products, high-cost products, low-cost products as part of your introductory series each time you launch something new using the backend sales flow chart. What they will not be receiving are the mails that you use to try and separate your list into one of these categories for the same reasons as with the lack of affiliate mailings as explained in the previous point.

Any of your customers that are not on your standard list will not be missing much in the way of making you money by not being there, because they are already where you want them, in a prime position to buy a premium product from you. In my experience, customers are more than ten times more likely to buy from you again than your standard list, and this is the reason I said that your list is the least targeted and lowest quality of the big five resources.

Customers to Long-Term Customers

Moving on swiftly, let's look at the probably the most important part here, and that is turning your customers into long-term customers, or big buyers. Now just because they are in this phase and have not bought your first high ticket item after standard follow-up procedures, does not mean they are useless, and will only ever buy the fifty-dollar products from you. Far from it, but it does mean one of three things. Either there was a gap in your marketing system that they fell through, whether it was your intro product, your ad copy, or your sales letter, or they could not afford to purchase the larger product, or finally they were not interested in what you had to offer.

For those reasons, you have to make sure to cater to all of them when you launch your next products. They will receive your small intro product, and as a follow-up to this they will also receive your larger high-ticket product. This is important here, because if they did not purchase your first high priced product, you will want to get them in at the bottom again before you do anything else and have them move through your intro product up to the bigger product. If your first time around was shoddy, they will know your game, and not buy into the second fresh new product line you have set up, and never move through to buy high-ticket items from you.

Now as a follow-up to this, you will want to also notify them directly about your high-ticket item sometime after you notify them of the intro product. This way, you are again regenerating the trust and the familiarity of your brand through your intro product and at the same time, having those that did not move up the ladder through your first product move up now. And of course, do not go thinking that people will be annoyed that bought the intro product to receive a bigger, better product later, again for the reason that your intro product is a real, and helpful product, not just a cheap excuse to sell bigger stuff. It is ethical, it covers all angles relating to your standard customers, and what is more, it works like a charm.

Turning Your Customers into JVs

Finally, turning your customers into joint venture prospects works in much the same way that you carried out for your list. You will also be pulling research numbers from these guys, and from that research you will know who to pull up for joint ventures. This is the only way to effectively do this and keep the joint ventures personal, instead of just mass mailing a list. It keeps you in the driver's seat. Of course, at this stage there is no other way to do this, chances are your list of customers who have purchased from you even though not as big as your list, will be too big to talk to all of them personally at this stage, which without this or affiliate stats, you have no other way of knowing who you want to make deals with.

What to Do with Your Customers Summary

Summing this up then, your customers are important to you and have a specific role. Changing that role at this all-important stage can do more harm than good. If you are going to contact them about anything other than research or sales of your products, refer to your research first and do it personally and individually for joint ventures, and avoid it altogether for turning them into affiliates. If you really want your customers to become affiliates as to plug the gap, make sure you have a higher commission integrated into the products they are buying from you, so they can take this offer up as a benefit if they are interested in the first place, and not to do it as afterthought.

Right, we are going to stop this one here as not to give you information overload. In next section, after the summary that follows, we will continue looking at how to cross your resources to get more out of them when we take a closer look at what to do (and what not to do) with your affiliates, long-term customers and joint venture prospects. We will also be taking a look at a few of the generalized ideas about treating all your lists correctly.

You will see exactly what effect this has later, but I can tell you now, that when you launch into this type of cross promotion of your resources, you will be drawing on all of this knowledge without having to wade through a bunch of text when you are busy launching your products and managing resources. It may seem a little strange right now, but I assure you, it is for the best, which you will be finding out for yourself very soon. See you in the next section!

Summary

❖ This whole section looks at cross promotion. Not as you may have been taught previously with other products, but this time, relating to the five resources you have been gathering. What we are planning to do now is quickly and effectively bring your resources together in unison and use the big five to multiply your promotion power many times over without having to ever bring any new resources in at all ultimately demonstrating how even if you have a small number of resources, you can outperform someone with the same number and quality of resources by up to twenty-five times.

❖ We are simply going to overlap each of them in a specific way so that each person becomes up to five times more profitable for you in five separate areas. What we will also be doing at the end of the next section is providing you with an additional diagram that you can add to the previous one to give a more complete outlook of the whole resource movement and development process.

❖ Let's begin by immediately looking at the pros and cons and the cross promotion of your list, turning your list into affiliates, customers, long-term customers and joint venture prospects.

- ❖ Your list. It is your first contact and your base promotion power that contains everyone that's ever passed through your site that has not qualified for a specialty list (i.e. bought something and landed themselves on the customers list, or singed up as an affiliate and landed on the affiliates list).

- ❖ They are all here, from freebie seekers to people that know what they have signed up for and those that do not, to those interested in your business, to those interested in following your progress and learning from you. It is generally the most numerous of all the resources and the lowest quality but is an essential starting point for filling the higher ranks.

- ❖ Keep in mind that it is not always profitable to expose one set of resources to another. This is especially true for your most valuable resources, for example, you would not make a strong effort to make your affiliates buy your product, because that is not their role, you end up losing profitable affiliates for the sake of a few thousand dollars of sales.

- ❖ So, let's get started with your list now. What do we want to turn your list into? Your list is there for one thing and one thing only, to increase the other four main resources. Turning your list into customers and long-term customers is straight forward, all it requires is simple list maintenance and regular promotion. Quite obvious this one, but there are a few more things that you can do with your list that many do not utilize.

❖ The first: Build your affiliate base and continue to build your joint venture base. Either of these that contain just one person that knows their stuff is more powerful than a list of ten or twenty thousand because of the power they have to make you (and themselves) profit compared to a lone ad of your own.

❖ This is why many successful and clued-up business owners are willing to use at least half of their list announcements for building their other resources, simply because it is more profitable. The sooner you can begin to see that it is far easier to make a lot of money from building resources instead of making sales, and act on this information, the sooner you will begin to make the real money.

❖ My point here is, especially with affiliate programs, if you have a high commission rate, (higher than the average 50-

55% that is) and a worth talking about seventy percent plus, do not be afraid to tell your list about it.

❖ So, whatever you do, do not think that gaining affiliates is all about that little button at the top of your sites with 80% for affiliates written in big letters. Hey, we spend money to promote free products to build our lists all the time, why cannot we do the same for our affiliates? Well, we can, and we do for the reasons we outlined above.

❖ So, the rule here is just this. If you are following the charts, we have put up for you, this guide or a modified version of it, built around your own needs, and your commissions are higher than the average fifty percent, go ahead and make sure people know about it through your promotion. Even consider making it a prime concern of yours to get these affiliates instead of the profits through sales of your big product if you have the choice.

❖ Now moving on and as far as turning your list into joint ventures goes, this is also very powerful but also open ended and variable, because it is hard to know exactly what people are capable of when they are approaching you from your mailings.

❖ Try not to regulate your JV partners to those who visit your site and individuals picked through top performing affiliates, because there is a lot of potential elsewhere, namely in your other resources.

❖ For example, an experienced marketer that subscribes to a selection of lists to keep up with what is going on around them, happens to subscribe to your list where you are selling an info product such as this. He will not buy your small how-to product, because he has got his system set up already and only promotes his own stuff to his list, unless it is a joint venture (this is very common among the big guys by the way), he will not buy your big product for the same reason, and he will not be joining your affiliate program for the above reason. He or she is a heavy hitter with a big list, but you are missing out. These are the people you are aiming to cater for here. It is not good if you are leaving massive holes like this, because you are missing out on some huge potential for profit.

❖ The problems with JVs at this stage is that they become kind of a lottery if you are not careful.

❖ You cannot just send out a mailing asking for anyone with a list of over ten thousand people to contact you for higher commissions, because then everyone else feels cheated and you may alienate some potential affiliates. In general terms, joint ventures should be a private thing, the deal will also vary from person to person, depending on your product, their list size, what they want in return and what you can grant in return. The best way to go about this is to keep it that way. Do not do a mass mailing just requesting joint ventures for the reasons above, we cannot do that for this particular resource.

❖ What I would suggest you do instead, which you should be doing with your list anyway, is carry on as your normally do, sending out your un-intrusive surveys to help with your research and find out as much info as you can about the people on your list, for something in return.

For example, a short valuable report that you have written on your area of expertise. In exchange you are getting vital info that not only allows you to tailor your ads to your list providing a better response rate, but at the same time you are building up a picture of who the good joint venture prospects are. Once you have done that, you can go through the results you have collected, and pick the top performers, the knowledgeable, and people with the most resources, and contact them individually.

❖ As you can see, your list is powerful, but not in the way most make out. Always remember your standard list is there to build your other resources, and is not only for making straight up sales, which is where most seem to misplace the power of this tool.

❖ Let's move on now to the less obvious resources beginning with your customers. Immediately we know from prior knowledge that your customers have bought from you before, they are more trusting of you and your products and are in my personal experience over ten times more likely to buy from you again than the standard list.

❖ Be careful here. This is where we need to look hard at the role the customers play, because they are more valuable than your standard list in many ways, and often less numerous. For these reasons we have to get it right, because un-subscriptions are far more devastating here than for your standard list. You did not spend all that time selling to them and building their trust just to scare them away again.

❖ So, in the natural flow of things, where do your customers go next? Onto long-term customers. As we discussed the added trust and stronger connection, and involvement makes it far easier to sell higher priced items to standard customers. When they buy a second product from you, they turn into long-term customers. They trust you, they spend often, and are likely to buy your products with the aim of profit in mind. Often, they will stay with you for years buying again and again. It is immediately clear that the wrong move here can hurt your profits hugely, because is where most of it is coming from.

❖ So, we already know the natural progression of things turns your customers into long-term customers, but what about the other resources? Well for a start, I always find it handy to already have your customers on your standard list. You will not need to make much effort getting them there, because it is likely they will have already subscribed to your stuff through your site, or the first product they purchased.

❖ This is useful, though, because you can demonstrate to them through offers to customers only that later reach the standard list that they are also on. I like to do this to emphasize my special offers for customers that have bought from me before are real, and the others do not get it, further increasing sales and enforcing trust. I would advise in addition to this to leave them on your standard list for this reason, as mailings to each resource should never be the same. Do not worry about making sure they are only on one list so you do not annoy them, they will be happy to see they are special in this way of receiving offers in special mails that the standard list will not get.

❖ Next up, affiliates. Do not mistake your customers for affiliates. Understanding their role is so important here. A mailing here or there attached to your offer mentioning commissions is fine but remember their role. They are here to buy your stuff and make you profit. More often than not they will either not know how to promote or are more interested in buying than promotion. Keep this in mind, and always tailor your mailings to the role the customers play and concentrate on turning them into long-term customers. If you try too hard to direct their attention to affiliate programs and promotion, you are alienating the people who want to buy from you and cutting off a main vein and one of the most important stages in actually making a profit at all.

- ❖ Finally, turning your customers into joint venture prospects works in much the same way that you carried out for your list. You will also be pulling research numbers from these guys, and from that research you will know who to pull up for joint ventures. This is the only way to effectively do this and keep the joint ventures personal, instead of just mass mailing a list. It keeps you in the driver's seat. Of course, at this stage there is no other way to do this, chances are your list of customers who have purchased from you even though not as big as your list, will be too big to talk to all of them personally at this stage, which without this or affiliate stats, you have no other way of knowing who you want to make deals with.

- ❖ In the next section, we will continue looking at these resources, and I'll show you how they begin to get even more powerful down the line compared to your list, often by hundreds of times.

❖ You will see exactly what effect this has later, but I can tell you now that when you launch into promotion, you will be drawing on all of this knowledge without having to wade through a bunch of text when you are busy launching your products and managing resources. You will be finding out for yourself very soon.

Overview of Resource Management

Part 2

❖ To continue to look at and discuss effective ways of controlling and using the resources that you are building through the launch of each product in such a way that you never have to worry about your promotion power ever again.

❖ To look at the reasons why many people cannot get such a system in place, and why it has not been working for them, and what you are doing differently to ensure it does work.

❖ To further discuss specific roles of each of your resources, allowing you more control over how you cross them over and have them build each other.

❖ To enhance resource management sections and complete the picture of list, affiliate, customer, joint venture and long-term customer management in such a way that's going to be highly beneficial to both your contacts, your business, and your pocket.

❖ To complete the sales system diagram by adding to it the flow of resources that will occur within your business when using this method.

❖ To sum up with a few pointers on how to treat each resource in general. Keep them happy, and how they will keep you earning.

Exponential Resource Management 2

In the last chapter, we looked at getting the most out of your five primary resources in such a way that they build themselves, but not just through other people promoting your stuff, but by the overlap of the resources through other means. We finished off talking about what to do with your standard customers, already having covered your list previously, so without further ado, we will now continue further down the resources and talk about the remaining three and what you should or should not be doing to make the most out of them. Please note, if you have not read the previous section, you should do so, as this will not make any sense otherwise and you will only get part of the picture.

What to Do with Your Long-Term Customers

Ok next up along the line of resources comes your long-term customers. At this point I would usually tell you about how important long-term customers are over something else, but as you may have noticed, they are all as important as each other, and you will have a hard time keeping numbers up effectively without a nice selection of each of the big five.

Long-Term Customers into Affiliates

So, let's take a look at what you are going to do with your long-term customers in regard to turning them into affiliates. Understand that when we talk about this, it may not be suitable to do so depending on your product. Turning any one of these resources into affiliates is especially important in the world of online marketing software or info selling, because after all, affiliate marketing is at least 20% of the whole picture. That is a huge chunk.

Well, after telling you that I am going to have to turn around now and tell you straight up that turning your long-term customers into affiliates, (or trying to) is a bad idea. Remember, these people have already spent their money with you, and have seen your affiliate offers several times. Many of them will be on your list receiving the ads for your affiliate program solely, as we talked about earlier. For this reason, there is absolutely no need to hassle these people directly with anything unnecessary.

Remember, this group has already spent a whole lot of money on your stuff, and if you want to keep them coming back, every time you contact them it has to be your best work. You need to be giving them something that they want, not just sending them ads, ads, ads. Also keep in mind, this particular list of yours should be the least numerous, but the biggest spenders.

Some of these people may come along to you and buy two-thousand-dollar product after two-thousand-dollar product.

You can immediately see how valuable they are.

You can also see through a little math how much more devastating it is to annoy anyone on this list or cause them to leave for any reason. Granted, you may argue there is plenty more out there, but this is where most of your advertising funds are going. Getting people to buy your products that are going to be bringing you in a mighty profit in the first place is not a short or easy task. Be very careful what you do with this list. This is going to be the long running theme in this section about your long-term customers.

Long-Term Customers into Your List

So, how about turning long-term customers into your list? Well, like I mentioned earlier, they are already on your list and most have generally followed the natural process of things, so there is no persuasion needed to that end. The problem comes when approaching them with your next products. What do you do?

Remember in effect these people are a list in themselves. Just think of them as your super high-quality list as opposed to your standard, high numbers low return one.

Again, be very careful what you do with these people, and if you do mail them, make sure they first know they are valued and give them something for free, also consider handing out discounts for future products, a reward scheme if you will, but remember to let them know why. Because they are valued. People like to feel valued, but if you do not tell them they are, then they are just going to assume you are another person, collecting more e-mail addresses, and sending them more ads.

Long-Term Customers Back into Customers

When it comes down to sending them ads when trying to sell them something else, things get a little more questionable. Do you start them in a system again, from the very beginning, or do you get them right in at the high-priced end? That is exactly what I want to touch on right now.

Turning your long-term customers back into customers that first will purchase an entry level product, then be sold onto the full product. Do you, or do not you?

Well, the answer is both a yes and no. I would suggest, for starters that you get them information out about your shiny new high-ticket product. This is a great way to start getting some feedback before the masses start promoting and coming through the system onto this high-priced product. Remember they have already spent their cash, and if your product was good, they already trust you and listen to you, and if your sales letter is good, you do not need to go through all that again, it serves no purpose.

The only time I would suggest that you start them from scratch all over again, is if it has been a long time since you have contacted them, or if you are going to be giving them something valuable for free therefore increasing the trust, and their feeling of special-ness further. For example, you have seen all those deals about people giving you bundles of stuff for free that is apparently supposed to be worth so much cash, so what is to stop you playing on that?

If you want to build trust with your long-term customers further, if your intro product plays too bigger part in your final high-ticket product further down the chain than you cannot afford to waive it, then give them your intro product. No, I am not talking about something free that was free anyway, I am talking take the $20-$60 out of your pocket that you are paying out in high commissions anyway from the intro product and give it to them.

How often have you been given something for free by someone you bought something off of only to see them selling it later as a real product? How special would you feel as a valued customer to pick this up and watch another ad come through on a standard list the same day selling the brand-new product you got free? Pretty special I would imagine. I should say if you have succeeded in general in creating a form of bond with these people, then they will start thinking you are worthwhile. It is not for us to decide who is worthwhile and who is not, it is the other way around. When this happens though, you will find more people start talking to you, mailing you, calling you, and some pretty interesting stuff happens, in the form of...

Long-Term Customers to JV Prospects

Turn your long-term customers into joint venture partners, small or large, long-term, or short term. Keep in mind that this is not by far your most effective way of generating joint ventures on a small scale, (ad swaps, list access, etc.) or even on a large scale (full blown partnerships of products, each playing a specialized role), however, you would be surprised what happens when you start talking to people.

This report for example would not even be here if it were not for that factor alone.

While we will not dwell on this for too long, I do want to make sure you understand I am not telling you to go out, and start spending your day talking to your customers, and as anti-professional as that sounds, we cannot strike conversations up with all these people, especially as your business starts developing over a number of products, the numbers can get a little overwhelming if you are going to try and pull something like that out of your hat.

What I do want to make sure you understand though is to look for those signs that the long-term customer that is contacting you would be a viable target for a joint venture offer, whether they mention they have a large list of their own, or on occasion you just get talking, and if it is with the right person, you might just find yourselves pulling some great ideas out of the bag together. Watch out for this, because it can, will and does happen more often than you may believe. I will not ramble on again at this stage about how important joint ventures are. Instead, let's move on to the next resource type in your arsenal.

What to Do with Your Affiliates

Now we are getting to the interesting stuff. Affiliates are up next, and after running through the do's and do nots of your paying customer base, things start to get a little more flexible here again, for simple reason that the situation is clear cut, and affiliates are more numerous than your long-term customer base for example. By clear cut, I mean you know what these people want. They are here solely to promote a good product, and make good money doing so. You do not need to carry out any research to confirm that one.

Now, as far as turning your affiliates' attention to your list, I am going to advise the same as previously just to make one hundred percent sure no one reading forgets that each of these resources should be a list in itself, with a clear goal, and a clear reason for being there. When you come to mailing them, you need to know what they want from you, as well as what you can give them in return. What we are not going to be doing in this particular case, is sending random adverts to your affiliates, not even for your products, because, as we learned earlier, they are more important than even your immediate profit, in fact, they are going to be the ones bringing in the majority of your new resources together with joint ventures (coming up next in the list).

We do however, get to send our affiliates ads of some sort, in fact very similar to the ads we talked about for your list, this time though, you are not trying to sell them on products to earn you hard cash, oh no, you are sending them ads to sell them on the promotion of you newest and latest products, not forgetting to mention to them how well your sales letter performs and giving them a nice visual picture of how much they can earn through your words. It might look different on the surface, but you are still selling them something, and all the rules you learn throughout this report apply to both monetary sales, selling free stuff, selling yourself and your products to gain joint ventures, or selling the potential to earn money through your affiliates. It is all about selling all the time.

That is enough covered to demonstrate my point, and we will take it further in a moment when we go on to talk about joint ventures.

Affiliates into Customers

Let's wrap up with the final three resources in affiliates section, starting with customers. How on earth do you get your affiliates to pay you as well as promote for you? Well, there is plenty of ways to turn these affiliates into customers.

The first you would think would be looking at the intro product and having affiliates that buy from you earn a higher commission. There is one problem with that though, what did we say the main goal of our intro product was not earlier on? if you remember we said that it is goal is not to make a profit, but to build your resources.

Charging affiliates cash to join up, whether it is single sale or membership using your intro product, is cutting off your nose to spite your face for this exact reason. This is especially true if you are attracting some heavy hitters and working in the online marketing info product world, not because they cannot afford to buy your product, but because it is just a hassle compared to going in, filling in a quick form, promoting straight away. If you have been following us so far, and your affiliate commissions are nice and high to get lots of people promoting, you will find that you will not be making much profit even if you did get them all to sign up. In any case, it is more likely you will put them off promoting and lose some quick blasts to some of these peoples big lists if you go about this any other way. Steer clear of it and remember the role of your intro products and the resource itself, your affiliates.

Affiliates to Long-Term Customers

Looking at affiliates in the light of converting them to long-term customers, however, is a different story altogether, simply because that is what your long-term product is there to do. Make you a profit, and if any of them sign up and buy this whilst promoting, while it will be very unlikely it will be mainstay source of customers for your business, it can be a nice little bonus. How you do this is only limited by the system you have set up, your imagination, adaptation, implementation. There really is no right or wrong way, and to list every single method would be a whole encyclopaedia in itself.

Let me give you some examples though so I do not leave you wonder what I am talking about. First example, you want to make a profit out of your affiliates, so along with your next ad to them about newest affiliate program you have released for your newest product goes an offer voucher for a discount, do not just want a boring old discount? Not a problem, how about the ticket only becomes valid when they have made five or ten sales.

Even better, instead of pushing affiliates hard, have the ticket only request one sale of your product before it becomes valid. It is very unlikely an affiliate with a good list is going to make exactly one sale when they blast an ad out. Easy they think, out goes the ad. Ten sales come in instead of the one that they needed. They get a discount or even a free product on top of their commissions.

At the same time, you persuaded someone to get out there and promote, not only bringing in more sales, but a bundle more resources that are going to do the same again and again. Best of all you were sleeping at the time. (I love that part)

Now ok granted you might be cringing at me right now wondering why I am telling you this, but let me say in my defence, first think about what you are selling. If it is a Sixty-dollar product, who cares if you give affiliates an 80% discount on top of their commission if they make a single sale. Remember that is not what we are talking about now. We are discussing high price items, anywhere from $500 to $10k per product. Now that discount starts to seem a little more significant and worthwhile. If I gave you 2k off one of my products on top of a 4k commission for making a single sale, would you blast an ad to your private, targeted list about that? There is a whopping wad of cash in it for you, and potentially hundreds more people for me to sell my products to for me.

It does not even have to go that far, even if you are only selling a $1250 product. When was the last time you were paid $500 per sale you made? If you have been paid that much before, I bet the product you were selling was pretty successful. Why do not more people pull stuff like this off? Simply wait until you have sold as many as you can in a short period of time, then open it up for affiliates with a deal like this, while the buzz is still there about your product.

Affiliates into JVs

Finally, in the affiliates resource crossing list, let's look at our final resource with a view to turn affiliates into a joint venture partner. This is really easy to do, and it is quick and painless for you. All it involves is either a simple phone call, or personal e-mail. Now we are getting into rare, does not happen every day, got to make this meeting as personal as possible territory.

What you are looking out for is a high rate of sales through your affiliate software. A simple search should do that if you have chosen a good system. Pick out the top two percent that have really made a dent and will generally make up the numbers big time and keep them handy. Not only should you have already rewarded them, but you should keep them ready and waiting for your next product, especially if it is related to your previous one.

If they did a good job promoting your previous product, it generally means they have the resources and ability to continue. You should be there when they decide that with a pre-empted contact prior to the release of your shiny new product, offering first stab at promotion, higher commissions than the norm. You may even be able to figure something else out if they have something you want. I cannot detail that here; every joint venture is different. Make of it what you need of it. The deal does not all have to be higher commissions and more money more money all the time.

If you could have anything right now that would move you towards your goals more quickly, or in an easier way, what is it? Does this person I am dealing with have it? If the answer is no, a safe bet is always the standard higher commissions. And remember, why are you giving them a load of special-ness over standard affiliates? Because they are valued affiliates. They probably know it already, but it does not half hit home when you say it, especially, as in the above example in the customers resource crossing section, when they see the standard offer going out to all the other affiliates (they will be on the same list still after all). That will sure show them that you are for real, they will not forget you either. Treat them right and they will continue to make you a whole load of money for many years to come and provide some really fruitful joint venture proposals and deals.

What to Do with Your JV Prospects

Talking of joint venture deals, let's move on now to the fifth and final section on crossing your resources over and talk about the do's and dont's of probably most lucrative marketing method in the business. Of the big five, your joint venture prospects and partners will likely be the least numerous of all your resources, but with the most stopping power per person. When you think that some of your JV's might end up being seen by lists of ten to a hundred thousand or more, it suddenly becomes clear how important this is. Let's look at where to take your joint ventures with regards to the other four resources, starting with affiliates.

Turning Your JVs into Affiliates

First up, you should keep in mind that most joint ventures that you receive after launching your fist two products will come from your affiliates anyway. As far as those who do not, they are really glorified affiliates only. As with difference between customers and long-term customers, you will find that even with those who are not your affiliates, you will be in contact with them pretty frequently anyway, whether they are on your instant messenger list, or you just fire emails at each other when you each launch new products.

Building up a circle of contacts that act in this way is extremely powerful in itself. Just, it takes a little more time to set up when it comes to product launches. Maintenance will not be a problem if you are using good affiliate software so, in this respect, keep your joint venture prospects separate. They are something special, and you will likely find yourself in contact with them even more so than your long-term customers, and they will be your first line of attack when launching future products. So when it comes to turning JVs into regular affiliates, do not bother, because they are all that and more already.

Turning Your JVs into Your List

Secondly, turning joint ventures into your list. Not something to dwell on, because your joint ventures should not be a list themselves.

They should be a selection of businesspeople that have access to resources that are beneficial to your business, not a bunch of e-mail addresses that you fire out ads to. Some may be on your list already, those that like to see what you are getting up to and when, and some may not. Either way, it does not matter, and you should never be thinking of your joint ventures as just a list of e-mail addresses. Things should be far more personal than that, at a cost of set up time to you, but producing some major profits and massive resource building potential.

Not Turning Your JVs into Customers

And now to the section I have been itching to tell you about, and that is moving joint ventures over to become your customers and long-term customers. It is possible that some may have bought from you before, or even learned how to promote from you if your products are geared towards that way of thinking, however, your joint venture partners are way too important to go advertising to unless it is in a 'hey check it out, thought you might find it interesting' kind of way.

Let me tell you a little story about how not to do this. I used to work with a few people when I first started, and we were getting along fine, we created a few sites, experimented, and compared notes a lot, and things were going great until I decided to branch out on my own. At regular intervals over the next three or four months whilst I was working on building my affiliate software, I started to receive interesting e-mails and messages from these people. Now understand that we were business colleagues, kind of like the people you talk to and hang around with and take your lunches with and had a laugh with at work.

Unfortunately, that all changed pretty quickly, and although I was still getting personal one on one deals from these people, they were trying to hard sell me. You can imagine logging on to the net and receiving mails or Instant Messages from one of your old friends that contained sales letter patter and hard sell messages. This is not how joint ventures are supposed to be carried out. It is inevitable, once you have been in contact with people for a period of time, you find yourself more relaxed and chatting more like friends, even though you both know business is the underlying subject.

So here's the deal, no matter how short of cash you get, no matter how much you think they are going to spend, do not hard sell or give your joint ventures sales pitches. Remember what they are there for, mutual deals that benefit both your products and businesses. Remember, this does not necessarily mean you cannot tell them about your new stuff or a new product someone has released but watch the way you go about it.

It is immediately obvious once you have been around a while when someone you know is trying to sell something to you in this manner. Sure, contact me, tell me about your new stuff, and show me the new opportunity you joined, tell me how it is going and what the word is on the net, ask me if I am interested in joining you, not a problem, but the moment you start talking to me about how much of a stunningly amazing deal I am getting, and how it is going to EXPLODE my sales by 400% overnight, guaranteed! Expect me to raise an eyebrow at you, turn around, and walk away. Moral of the story, watch what you are saying and how you are saying it if you want to keep your joint venture partners close.

The Final Diagrams

Alright, do you now see how each resource can go on to become relevant in two sections, double the promotion power for you, but at the same time you have to be very careful not to go over the top, or make a wrong move when trying to cross your resources over. Some of the above are obvious and will lose you your resources in a particular way, and some of the less obvious have time-based constraints which as pointed out in the relevant sections, and will have you messing with confusing tangled balls of resources that are not viable compared to the amount of profit they bring you. Before moving on to three general rules about treating your customers correctly, here is the chart to demonstrate in note form what we have just talked about above and previous chapter for each of your resources.

Note: This is not some fancy marketing system that has been created for the sake of doing so. It simply demonstrates one of the fundamentals of every manual I have ever written. Your resources, and how when they are building each other, you can never say you have no one to promote to, no one to promote your stuff, no one to strike deals with, and no way to make profit, because you do have all of those things. It is all here, ready and waiting.

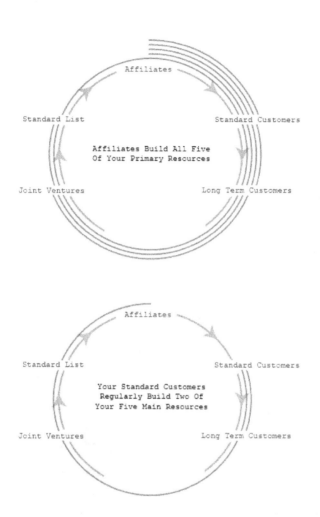

Affiliates

Standard List   Standard Customers

**Affiliates Build All Five
Of Your Primary Resources**

Joint Ventures   Long Term Customers

Affiliates

Standard List   Standard Customers

**Your Standard Customers
Regularly Build Two Of
Your Five Main Resources**

Joint Ventures   Long Term Customers

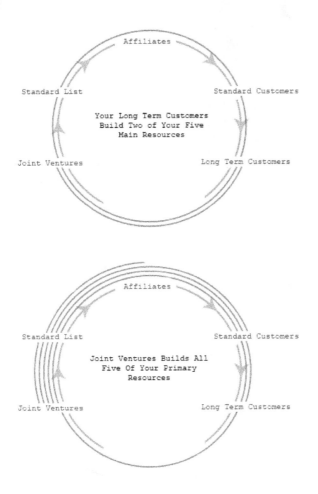

Affiliates

Standard List   Standard Customers

**Your Long Term Customers
Build Two of Your Five
Main Resources**

Joint Ventures   Long Term Customers

Affiliates

Standard List   Standard Customers

**Joint Ventures Builds All
Five Of Your Primary
Resources**

Joint Ventures   Long Term Customers

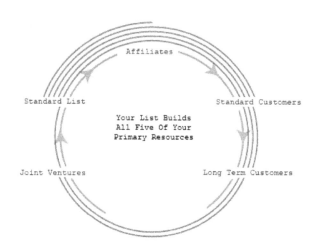

Affiliates

Standard List

Your List Builds
All Five Of Your
Primary Resources

Standard Customers

Joint Ventures

Long Term Customers

3 Steps to a Good Customer Relationship

Ok, finally before moving on to the next subject, and wrapping up this section, I would like to talk to you about three, very general concepts relating to how to and how not to treat your customers, with a view to getting the most out of each every one of them through your marketing.

I would like to start off by giving you a quick rundown of freebie syndrome and giving away the world.

Freebie syndrome, as I call it, unfortunately seems to be almost incurable over short periods of time. This occurs when you give too much for too little to your resources. Generally, the people that do this are in the mindset that people will remember them, thank them, like them for giving things to them. It is important, however, that no matter what resource you are dealing with not to do this too regularly for starters, and secondly do not give away anything worth more than around sixty dollars at the absolute max, especially when the product is new.

If you find yourself starting to do this, whether it is with affiliate commissions, mailings to your list, or being too kind to your customers or even your joint venture prospects and contacts, you will likely see that they start to take it for granted and come to expect it, only to suddenly be offended when you do not keep up the pattern. Remember this if you are giving freebies away, make sure people know that it is a special thing that you do not do very often. This not only adds even more value to your words and products, but inoculates against freebie syndrome from the start, and you will not have to keep giving away the world to keep everyone happy.

Lastly, and quite simply, keep in touch. I am not suggesting you mail your resources every day, or even every week, but I would suggest keeping in contact at least three or four times a month minimum without making that fatal mistake of sending out e-mails when you have nothing to say. If you do not do this, gradually, over time, people will forget that trust you have built up with them, or even worse, forget who you are altogether, or not remember to update their accounts and subscriptions with their new contact details.

Wrapping Up

Generally, they are more likely to remember you the further down the resource chart they are, and the more you should be doing to make sure they stay this way. That about wraps it up for how to treat your customers. I hope you will agree that we have just talked through something far more important than customer service techniques here. We have just covered how to get your resources to build each other internally. Couple this with the external building and the influx of new customers you are receiving through your new products, and you will find yourself in an abundance of promotion power.

BONUS

The Traffic "INFERNO" Strategy

Introduction

I would like to congratulate you. Granted, some of the traffic tips we are about to give you probably will not make you millionaires overnight. They may not even be that easy to implement.

But...

They WILL give you that tasty edge you need over your competition – these will be things that your competition has not even thought of.

Take the material very seriously and make it your #1 goal to test before passing judgment.

Once upon a time on the web, any traffic was good traffic. If you got a lot of traffic, you could make money somehow – by selling products, selling advertising, or selling impressions. With big traffic, you were riding high. You were the proud owner of some very valuable Internet real estate.

Back in the old days, even if you did not get a lot of traffic, you could reasonably expect one-half to one percent of your visitors to do SOMETHING when they got to your site. They'd either buy something, click on a banner, sign up for your opt-in list, or click on an advertiser's link.

But those glory days are gone. The last couple of years have shown that any old traffic is not only worthless, but it can also cost you money. There is nothing like racking up bandwidth charges month after month without seeing a single affiliate commission check. It is sad but true: in theory, your web site could have a phenomenally high Google page rank, be one of Alexa's top sites, get half a million visitors a month... and lose money.

There is only one kind of traffic worth a pixel in today's Internet marketplace. TARGETED TRAFFIC.

So that is what this Affiliate Classroom Special Report is all about: 10 powerful and underutilized ways to generate TARGETED traffic.

As you will discover, many of these tips are not for marketing wimps. A few are free. But most require at least a minimal cash investment. And they all require you to develop a rare but powerful online business skill – imagination.

Yes, you will have to wrap your brain around your site topic and the products you are trying to sell. That's what "targeting" requires – being selective. You have to know not only the kind of visitors you want, but the kind of visitors you DO NOT want.

Paying for Links

The reciprocal link principle is simple – find websites with good rankings and plenty of traffic, and trade links with them. But when you are just starting out, why should a big important site give a little upstart like you any kind of link at all?

At Affiliate Classroom we like to say that there is only one way to find out – ASK. It helps if you have some kind of relationship with the site owner. But even if you do not, you can sometimes use the time-honoured principle of bribery to get a link from a well-ranked site.

Ask for a link. If you get turned down, say "Would you consider linking to me for $100?" You would be surprised at how many webmasters will take you up on your offer!

This technique works best with privately owned sites that rank in the top 10 for targeted keywords in niche markets. There is no point in trying to get a link from Kiplinger's or Newsweek's or Vogue's web site. But if you are selling weight loss products, and $50 will buy you a link from a small web site that is ranked #1 for "low-carb dessert recipes," you are probably better off buying that link than buying $50 of PPC advertising. This also cannot hurt your own search engine ranking.

Make sure you have a simple written agreement about exactly what the link will say (you want your keywords in it) and the duration of the link – 6 months, a year, forever, etc.

A similar technique involves finding all the sites that link to your competitors and offering them a cash incentive to add your link to their site. You can find these sites by going to Google and typing in "link:www.yourcompetitorslink.com.

Get Listed On Coupon And Special Offer Sites

There are dozens of special offer, coupon, and rebate sites online today. Simply go to Google and type in "coupon sites" and you will see what we mean. "Coupon" is searched at least a few hundred thousand times a month. Some smart folks are getting a lot of traffic with simple sites that are just lists of links to various sites with special offers.

How can this help YOU get targeted traffic? The people who visit these sites are looking for a discount, a deal, a freebie, a rebate, or a bargain. If you can offer some kind of special bonus – whether it is a cash rebate, a physical or digital product, or a service – you can ask to be included on these sites.

As long as you can come up with an offer that qualifies, you will get accepted. If you wish, you can create several web pages, each with a slightly different special offer, and see what makes the most sales.

Very few affiliate marketers are taking advantage of this. Yes, it does mean you have to create a little something extra for the people who buy through these sites. You will have to track their purchases. But considering that you will also be getting incoming links from some very highly ranked web sites, it is worth the little bit of extra work.

Old Fashioned Business Networking

Yes, even though we are all buried in Spam, it is still possible to make new business contacts online. The recent JV (Joint Venture) craze reflects the simple principle that in the end, people do business with PEOPLE – not with pixels, bits, and bytes.

Old fashioned networking is still alive and well online. And it is the best method for getting some good exposure if you are just starting out and have no money for marketing. By building strong business relationships, you will soon have other marketers offering to link to you, publish your articles, write about your site in their newsletter, and even offer you free advertising.

One of the best places to make business contacts in your field is in forums. For example, if you have started an affiliate web site that sells specialty dog training devices, hang out in the many dog-related forums and newsgroups. But instead of trying to help end consumers so they will visit your site, make friends with experts in related fields. In this case pet sitters, groomers, dog trainers, veterinary assistants, even animal behaviourists can all be excellent contacts.

As with all business networking, look for ways to help your colleagues. If they have their own site, offer them a link on yours. If they have an opt-in list, perhaps you can set up a special web page, and give them a rebate on any commissions you make. If they write their own articles, perhaps you can turn them into a mini-ebook and offer it to all your visitors.

And there is no reason you cannot be proactive and send an email to non-competitors – or even competitors – whose sites you admire. You do not have to consider every competitor your enemy. In a future special report, we will explain exactly how you can create powerful partnerships with your competitors. But for now, simply look for opportunities to be helpful.

One easy way to help – provided you do it diplomatically – is to point out a problem on someone's site or in their ezine. If you find a broken link or some other error, drop them a note. Most webmasters WANT to know if a link suddenly stops working or if their database is generating internal server errors.

Another way to make powerful friends online is to read your Spam. That is because ALL online merchants want to know if someone is promoting their affiliate product via Spam. It is not just the Spammer who can suffer some stiff legal penalties – they can too. So, if you see someone's eBook or software being sold via Spam, write to them, and let them know. Make sure you keep the original Spam and send it to them as an attachment (not forwarded) so they receive all the headers intact.

How can networking help get you targeted traffic? If you make 20 strong, personal, one-on-one business contacts every month, at least five of them will end up sending you traffic. Somehow, someday, they will start pushing the right kinds of visitors to you.

It might be by linking to you. They may mention your site in a viral eBook or one of their articles. They might want to do a joint venture or partner on a money-making project. They might do all these things – and many more. Yes, it is old fashioned. It is not autopilot. It is not passive. But networking costs you nothing except time – and can be worth gold in the long-term.

Exploit The Handheld Market

This one is outrageously simple, yet almost completely overlooked. Next time you create a viral information product of any kind – whether it is an eBook, a special report, a white paper, a case study, or a compilation of articles – get it formatted for handhelds.

There are dozens – perhaps even hundreds – of sites that offer free downloads for handhelds. And most handheld users are always on the lookout for something to read on that little screen.

It will cost less than $50 to pay someone from Guru.com, Elance.com, or Scriptlance.com to format your product for the handheld market. And with over 11 million handheld users out there, that is a lot of potential viral traffic for your site.

Combine Surveys and Polls With PPC

You probably already know that surveys are excellent for finding out what your target market wants. But if combined with low cost, quick and dirty Google PPC, surveys can also send lots of targeted prospects to your site every month.

First, do some keyword research. You will need to find keywords and key phrases that are related to your survey topic but do not have too many Google campaigns running. You can do this very quickly with a tool like Jeff Alderson's AdWords Analyzer, since it will show you exactly how many Google campaigns are running for various keywords at any given time.

Second, sign up for an inexpensive survey service like Survey Monkey (www.surveymonkey.com). We do not recommend free survey services, since they tend to limit the number of participants, and the whole point is to get as many people as possible to take your survey. Now design a survey that will appeal to your target market.

Next, come up with an incentive for people to take your survey. Make it a download, so you can capture the prospect's email address. And make it viral. Even a simple white paper can be viral. You do not necessarily have to cram it with affiliate links. Just make sure your URL is conspicuously listed on every page.

Now put up a simple web page that introduces people to the survey topic, offers the incentive, asks for an email address where you can send the download link and the survey results, and links to the survey.

Finally, use at least a dozen of the keywords your researched earlier to set up Google AdWords campaigns advertising your survey. Make sure the ad uses your keyword, and that it mentions the incentive. "Take this photography survey, get a free gift." You do not have to be the #1 ad. You can even be on the second or third page.

The point is to capture a targeted prospect's contact information for a very small investment. But there are some additional serious fringe benefits in addition to traffic.

First, you will collect valuable information on what your prospects are looking for.

Second, you will have their permission to contact them with the survey results and the download link for the thank you gift. And third, if you make that free gift a viral report, you will eventually get more targeted traffic. Nice!

You can do a variation of this with a simple one question poll. Everything else is the same, except you will want to come up with an intriguing question for the poll – something that will pique people's curiosity about the results.

And if you want to pass on the free report incentive and try something different, why not enter every participant in a drawing for a valuable prize of tangible goods? Make it a prize with a high perceived value, worth at least $100. Now you have an excuse to collect snail mail addresses of your targeted visitors – a perfect way to build an in-house direct mail list, so you can take advantage of the ideas in #10 of this report.

New Fashioned Link Strategies

It has been true since the birth of the World Wide Web: people like pages of useful links. They will bookmark them and return to them. And today, because links are so important to search engine rank, link pages should be part of every targeted traffic plan. Old fashioned link pages are the ones you build by hand, painstakingly, over many months and years. These are annotated links pages that include not only a URL, but a brief description of the site and its contents. These "handmade" link pages take a lot of time and a lot of effort. Frankly, they are slowly dying out on the web.

But thanks to web-based services and innovative software, you can build useful pages of links while enjoying all the search engine benefits – and without all that painstaking labour. Every serious affiliate marketer should I think about creative ways to take advantage of these "new fashioned" link strategies.

One simple new-fashioned strategy is to set up a links page through a service like Bravenet. With this type of page, webmasters fill in a form to "apply" for a reciprocal link with you. On this page, you can explain that the application is subject to review, and that you will only link to them if they have ALREADY linked to you.

You can also include required text for the link they give you – you definitely want your keywords or your "brand name' in that link! And you can even set up a response email, which can be customized. This response email should ask everyone who applies to send you the full URL of the page where they have got your link.

But do not stop there. Once a webmaster sends you the URL where your link appears, submit that link to Google. Just go to www.google.com/addurl.html, fill in the form, and add the page with your link. Submit it to any other relevant search engine or directory. You want those search engines to know that page exists so they can spider it as fast as possible.

After you have accepted the other webmaster's link, it will get added to your custom link page. So, make sure your links page gets added to your site map. In fact, make sure you link to it from EVERY page of your site.

Give Away Unrestricted Resale and Reprint Rights

This traffic idea is simple, obvious, and still enormously underutilized. The idea is simple:

❖ Create short eBooks or special reports on highly specialized topics that would be appeal to your target market.

❖ Add your URL to every page in a header or footer, as well as on the title page and at the end of the book.

❖ Then give away unrestricted, unlimited reprint and resale rights to the ebook for FREE.

"Wait," you say, "has not this been done before?" Yes, to a certain extent. It has been exploited by some info product creators, especially the how-to-make-money-online crowd and the motivational gurus.

But your average affiliate marketer selling hard goods, software, and services to niche markets rarely uses this idea to its full potential. Let's look at an example.

Imagine you have built a killer affiliate web site that specializes in bridesmaids dresses. What kind of viral eBook could you possibly create? How about some special reports on...

- 20 extra special "finishing touches" for the bridesmaids' face, hair, nails, lips, etc.

- The most popular colours in bridesmaids dresses for each season of the year.

- A dozen unique ideas for bridesmaids gifts.

- 10 ways to make the big day special for the bridesmaids, too.

- 100 online wedding resources (from music to Victorian weddings to tuxedos etc.).

- 50 love poems and biblical scriptures you can read at your wedding (from public domain sources).

- Creating a wedding scrapbook.

- 25 toasts to the bride and groom for the nervous best man.

- 5 creative ways to preserve and display your wedding invitation.

All these viral products relate to the topic of your site. They have a high perceived value, and would make excellent bonuses, freebies, or incentives on wedding-related web sites. Most can be created with a minimum of effort. And all these topics should have a long shelf life – not a few weeks or months, but years and years.

If you tell the world that they can take these viral reports and do anything they want with them – including sell them on Ebay – you may suddenly end up giving away hundreds, even thousands of copies. Can you say "viral?"

Combine Dumb PPC Advertising With Smart Virals

All PPC beginners make the same mistake. They "discover" a very popular keyword on a very popular topic that gets thousands of searches... but only three Google campaigns! They can barely contain their excitement as they write their ads and put in their bid for six, seven, eight, or even ten cents a click.

And low and behold, soon they start getting clicks – lots of them! They even make a few sales. Then a few more. And they breathe a sigh of relief when they see that their CTR (click through rate) is slightly above Google's stated "acceptable" rate.

Until they get an email from Google's Adwords Support, saying that their keyword is in danger of being disabled because the CTR is not high enough.

It is upsetting, it is frustrating, and it may not even be fair or ethical. But Google, for reasons not entirely known, will sometimes require impossibly high clickthrough rates for certain keywords. Instead of a CTR of .5%, suddenly a CTR of 8%, 10% or even 15% is not good enough.

Emails to support, begging for guidance or clarification, prove futile. Bye-bye keyword. It is dumb to try and salvage campaigns based on these keywords. You tweak your ads over and over, raise your bids, and waste days trying to divine Google's required CTR. Experienced PPC advertisers know that it is almost impossible to keep one of these campaigns alive once Google starts to raise the stakes.

However, there is a way you can grab a large amount of targeted traffic, if only for a limited time, by intentionally running these dumb campaigns. It will not work for every niche since these types of keywords are not common to all topics. And if you suddenly find yourself struggling with a campaign like this, pause it long enough to put this strategy in place.

First, you have got to locate a fairly general keyword that gets a lot of searches but has fewer than 10 Google campaigns. Software like Adword Analyzer is useful for this, but it will still take some digging. The best way to locate a good candidate is to run Adword Analyzer searches on extremely broad terms. The keyword "book," for example, only has a handful of Google campaigns running at any given time yet is searched over a MILLION times a month. "Kelly blue book" is the same way.

Next, create an unlimited, unrestricted reprint and resale rights info product (see #7 above) that might appeal to people who search on a term like "Kelly bluebook." Chances are that these folks are either buying or selling a used car. So, develop an ebook of resources, tips, warnings, or other useful information on buying or selling used cars. Make sure the information will have a long shelf life.

Then run a "dumb" Google campaign on "Kelly blue book," offering your report for free. Make sure the landing page states boldly, in no uncertain terms, that people can sell or give this book away anywhere and everywhere – even on Ebay.

Now sit back and watch the traffic come in. Google probably will not let that campaign run for very long – at least not at .06 a click, and probably not at 20 times that. But with a little luck, you will probably be able to give away at least a hundred ebooks before Google disables the keyword. Even if you gave away only 20, it cost you only a few bucks.

And you never know what kind of future life that viral report will have. It may become a free bonus in a bestselling package. It may end up being distributed on hundreds of car sites all over the web. Some online marketer may feature it as a brilliant example of viral marketing. It may even get talked about in a car magazine.

Get Links on Thank You and Confirmation Pages

Another technique available to almost everyone but exploited by a mere few. You probably already know about putting links to your site or products on your Thank You pages, Confirmation pages. You may even put links to specific affiliate products on these pages.

But have you ever considered approaching OTHER sites and asking for a link on THEIR Confirmation and Thank You pages? You may be surprised at how many webmasters of specialized content sites would be delighted to offer you space on one of these pages – especially if you offer them an incentive, like a cash payment, a plug in your ezine, or a free sample of your product.

A variation of this involves "404 Error" pages. If you find a site that you feel could send you good, targeted traffic, ask if they would like a sample of your product in return for letting you create a custom 404 error page for them. It can be a simple page with just a few links: one back to their home page, one to yours, and one to some kind of special discount offer or other incentive on your site.

This technique works best with sites that are non-commercial in nature. There are thousands of sites, created and maintained by enthusiasts of all sorts, that are not designed to make money. Many blogs fit into this category. They may be about a hobby, a religion, a sport, or an idea. They may exist just for fun. They may be a venue for someone's original stories or poetry.

But if their owners have access to their server, and create their own pages, you may be able to "bribe" them into sending you targeted traffic by sharing a bit of unused space with your links or offers.

Offline Advertising

Have you ever wondered why some of the biggest online businesses spend huge sums on direct mail, as well as TV, magazine, radio, and newspaper advertising? Is it because they have money to burn?

No, it is because mass media ads and direct mail can actually draw highly targeted visitors – prospects who are ready to buy. Those big companies with deep pockets use mass media ads to create indelible name recognition in the public's mind. After branding their company into our consciousness, they use direct mail techniques such as postcard mailings to send offers to hand-picked prospects who are most likely to make a purchase soon.

It is strange, but very few online marketers have discovered the power of direct mail. A handful have learned to use classified advertising – the distant cousin of expensive mass media advertising. But almost none are using other forms of offline ads. This can also give you an enormous edge. If you make your living from affiliate programs and related upsells, you can bet that your competition is not doing any sort of offline advertising.

If you think offline advertising is too expensive, think again. Because PPC has become so popular, the cost of high-quality online advertising is rising dramatically. It is common for a PPC campaign in a competitive field to cost $1 or more per click – sometimes much more. And you do not even know if those clicks are coming from real prospects or your competitors' itchy fingers.

In fact, today PPC can actually end up costing as much, or more, than direct mail on a cost per sale basis. So do the math before you write off direct mail. A mailing of custom colour postcards, for example, can definitely cost less than $3 each to print and mail, and that includes the mailing list.

More importantly, you must think about your projected COST PER SALE when comparing PPC and direct mail. Clicks may be cheap, but customers may not. All traffic – whether targeted or not – is made up of people. If these "clickers" are unlikely to be buyers, you will lose money on PPC no matter how cheap the clicks are.

For highly competitive keywords you can easily end up paying over $3 per click if you want to be on the first page of Google. If you stop and consider WHO you are selling to, the direct mail campaign may be a better investment. You can target exactly the sort of person you want, with just the right demographics, and tell them to go to your site where you will show them an irresistible offer.

What about classifieds? With classified print advertising, you can advertise your URL in literally hundreds of small daily newspapers for ridiculously small amounts per ad. And classified ads in major national niche magazines can be very affordable – and usually pull extremely well.

These days, television ads may not even be out of your reach. If you enjoy the spotlight, you can purchase "leased access" time on local U.S. cable television. By Federal Law, every local cable station must allow the general public to purchase time on their channel, in blocks of 30 minutes. Since the costs are also controlled by law, even in large metropolitan areas a 30-minute segment may cost as little as $200.

These days, $200 will not buy you much PPC in a competitive field like mortgages or debt management. You do not even have to be selling to a local market to make a television segment pay. As long as you have got an easy-to-remember URL, put a special television offer page on your site. Then offer a high value upsell free to the first 20 people who respond to the "TV special."

Finally, do not forget other incredibly simple offline methods of getting your URL out there. Instead of a traditional business card, print several thousand with your URL in huge letters and leave them anywhere relevant. Do not forget pencils and pens, letter openers and coasters, calendars, and T-shirts...

Remember, you do not need a bricks and mortar location to use offline advertising.

Amazon, Gateway, Dell, AOL, and many other online businesses spend millions on offline promotional methods. That is what has made their brands and URLs famous.

You can do the same on a much smaller scale. It is a big offline world. Plenty of people spend more time offline and on. Open your mind to using offline marketing to get your message in front of the RIGHT people. That way you can get your URL in front of targeted prospects. And when they visit your site, they have actually made a conscious decision to do so.

CPSIA information can be obtained
at www.ICGtesting.com
Printed in the USA
BVHW062003250321
603411BV00002B/145